Mr. Fox's Climate Change Inventions

Written and Illustrated
By Connie Bintner

To Larry Rosier,
my brother and inventor,
who inspired me.

To Bob,
my husband, who encouraged me
throughout my life.

Fossil fuels, oh my, so wrong.
They cause pollution in the air.
Oh my, can this be my sad song?
Today, I want to find a way
To make a better place to stay.
Mr. Fox invented, you'll see,
Devices which make power free.
No electric lines go to homes.
Cars will run for free on their own
Without a fossil fuel at all.

The first to come in fossil fuels
A hard plant fuel that's known as coal.
Deep down in earth men took their toll.
They breathed the air that caused black lung.
They cough at mines and at the plant.
Someone do something about that!

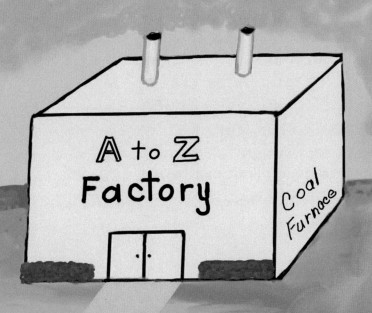

Railroad cars carry the black coal
To electric plants far and wide.
At the plant the black coal is burned.
This smoky smog they cannot hide.
Stop coal to fire their furnaces.
Pollution can be stopped and turned.
Use Mr. Fox's charging tools
And electric generators.

7

smoke from natural gas

Natural Gas Rig

Electricity

made with coal from power plant

Natural Gas

Natural Gas

Deep in earth natural gas and gasoline

Groceries | Toys | Coffee | Dental | Nails | BANK

The electricity that's made
Goes to the businesses and homes.
How can black coal become archaic?
The answer is Fox's device
Which makes its electricity
Possible wherever one roams.

Use Fox's Electric Power

Other fossil fuels to fear
Are gasoline and natural gas.
Pollution's in the air! Oh dear!
Take gas from cars and trucks! NOW!
Stop climate change on earth for US!
Electric Fox's cars are how.
Clean air to save the planet.

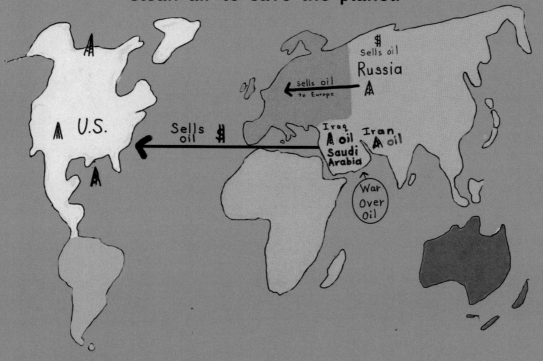

**No more
Smog from
Gas pollution**

No more
Expensive gas for
Cars and Trucks

Oil Slick

Oil and Natural Gas

Oil rigs on shores sometimes get hit
By raging storms that take their lick.
Birds and animals get oil slick
On feathers and on fur on shore.
No need for this if oil is stopped—
With a new electric device
To run future electric cars.

10

Pipelines of oil cause great alarm.
They may break from cold or earthquakes.
Oil then scatters to make huge harm
To plants and wild beasts in its wake.
We do not need this vast mistake.

When oil wells need a helping hand,
Water is put down in the pipe
Causing oil to come up with hype.
This kind of fracking should be banned.
It ruins the water on this land.
The rock plates shift to cause earthquakes.
No need for fossil fuels this type.

Water poured down the pipe to flush out the last oil in the ground.

Oil in Water Supply

Oil and Water

Oil in Water Supply

We want clean water

No more earthquakes

Clean Up Water

Natural gas, a fossil fuel,
Heat homes in the cold of winter.
But now there is a breaking rule,
Fox's electric power's new!
Natural gas is less in view.

No need for
fossil fuels.
No oil
No coal
No natural gas
No solar
No hydro-
electric
No coal-powered
electricity
No wind power
No atomic power

Mr. Fox's
Electric
Generator
warms homes
and
produces
electricity

It seems that nuclear power
Can have wastes too hard to dispose.
Leaks in the reactor tower
Causes people to form cancer.
Fox's power is the answer.
Eliminate the NUKES—right now!

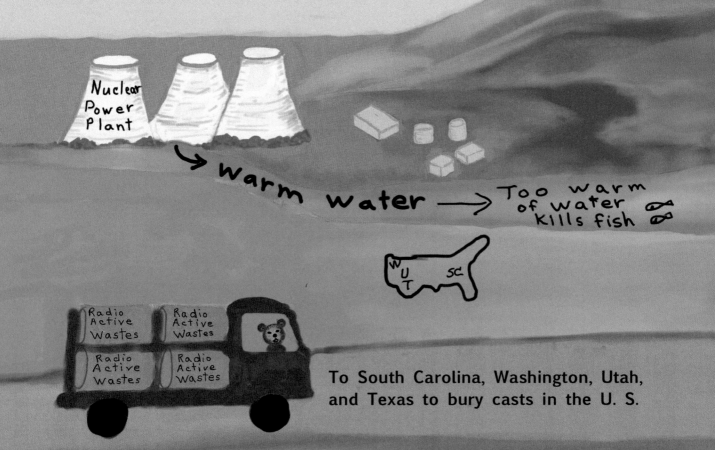

To South Carolina, Washington, Utah, and Texas to bury casts in the U. S.

Site of worst atomic reactor failure.
Most toxic in the world

14

Burying Casts of Toxic Wastes

Car's smoke goes up to ozone high.
Breaking holes way up in the sky.
The warmth grows all over the world.
Climate change melts the permafrost.
A house built on permafrost sinks.
Lakes appear where the house once stood.
Owners relocate if they could.
Mr. Fox's cars don't pollute.
This can stop climate change for good!

Glaciers melt at alarming rates.
Smoke and pollution cause this fate.
People, animals, and plants need
Glaciers' water on which to feed.
Fast melting icebergs cause flooding.
Shores will move inland when ice melts.
When melting glaciers are not there,
Now climate change is everywhere.

Global Climate Crisis

2020

2010

2000

1990

1980

What is
happening
to the
glaciers?

1970

1960

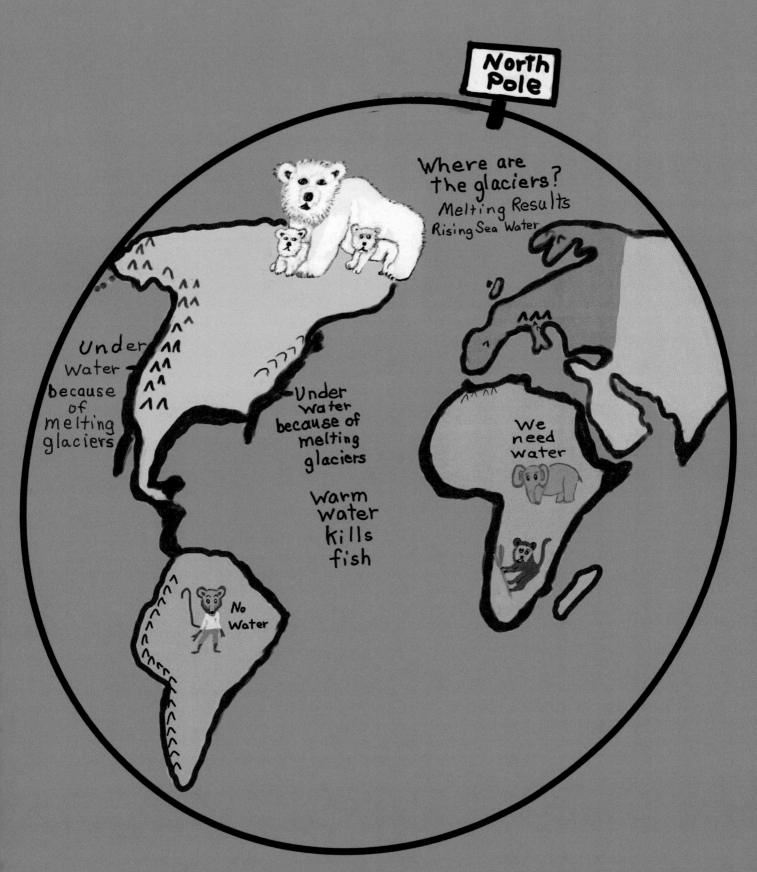

Mr. Fox can change the whole world.
His new electricity's goal,
No need for fossil fuels like: coal,
Gasoline, and natural gas.
Powers not needed now in mass
Are: wood, solar, hydro, thermal,
Atomic, windmills, and tidal.

Coal

Natural Gas

Gas

Hydro

Solar

Wind mill

Atomic

Thermal

Wood

Heat

Tidal

Not Needed

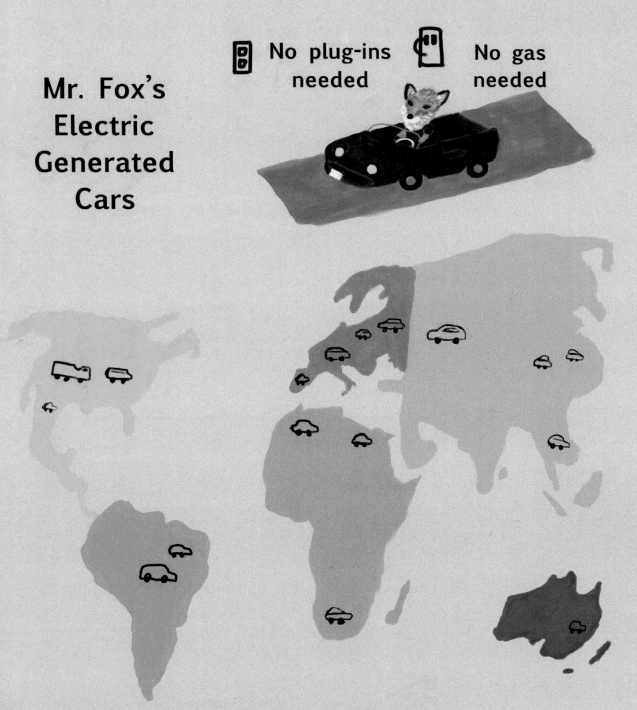

Mr. Fox's Electric Generated Cars

No plug-ins needed

No gas needed

His electric cars will be sold.
All over the world, I am told.
The people will buy gas no more.
Electric plug-ins not needed.
Pollution from cars depleted.
Climate change will be stopped on earth.

Russia

Oil For Sale

Middle East Oil

Middle East won't export their oil.
Need for oil will be depleted.
Middle East wars took their grim toll.
Use Fox's recharging device
Or electric generator.
They'll not pollute in any state.
What a climate change this will make!
The happy earth will take a break.

Plastic bottles, oh what a sin!
Oceans filled with plastics—how grim.
Those plastics made have oil within.
They won't degrade in years to come.
What in this wide world can be done?
Now climate change begins with you.
Use less plastics and recycle.

Climate change we will stop right now
With Mr. Fox's devices.
His electricity will reign:
In houses, factories, airplanes,
Cars, ships, machinery, and trains.
Leaving behind oil rigs, windmills,
And coal factories of no use.
Solar panels and gas stations
Will be obsolete—what good news!
His electric generators
And his great charging devices,
Will rule all over the nation.

Mr. Fox's
Electric
Generator
Device

Mr. Fox's
Charging
Device

Auto factories will start up
A new kind of electric car
Which recharge themselves while driving.
This kind of car will up the bar!
Over the world, they will be riding
In Fox's new electric cars.

Homes make own electricity
With Mr. Fox's new device.
He can power the big cities,
Farms, villages, and deserts, too.
Then climate change can come to you.

24

What a wonderful world it'll be!
No pollution in air to see.
No windmills, or atomic plants,
Nor smoke stacks from electric plants.
No solar panels in the sun,
Nor oil refineries to run.
No plastic jars or straws recalled.
No coal is being used at all.

Clean air

No plastic straws

Clean
Water

Mr. Fox's inventions told
Of engineer's ideas, bold.
In every room inventions stood.
To advertise was what he should.
In a car, the first device went.
Over the world, the message sent.
Life was changing for the better.

26

Fox is an inspiring genius!
He mastered a charging device
That changed the world so that it can
Outwit the polluting oil man.
Fox's devices, put in cars,
Can make it go forever far.
His electric generators, you see,
Will light the world's houses for free.

Autos Run Forever

No Need for Plug-Ins

No Need for Gas

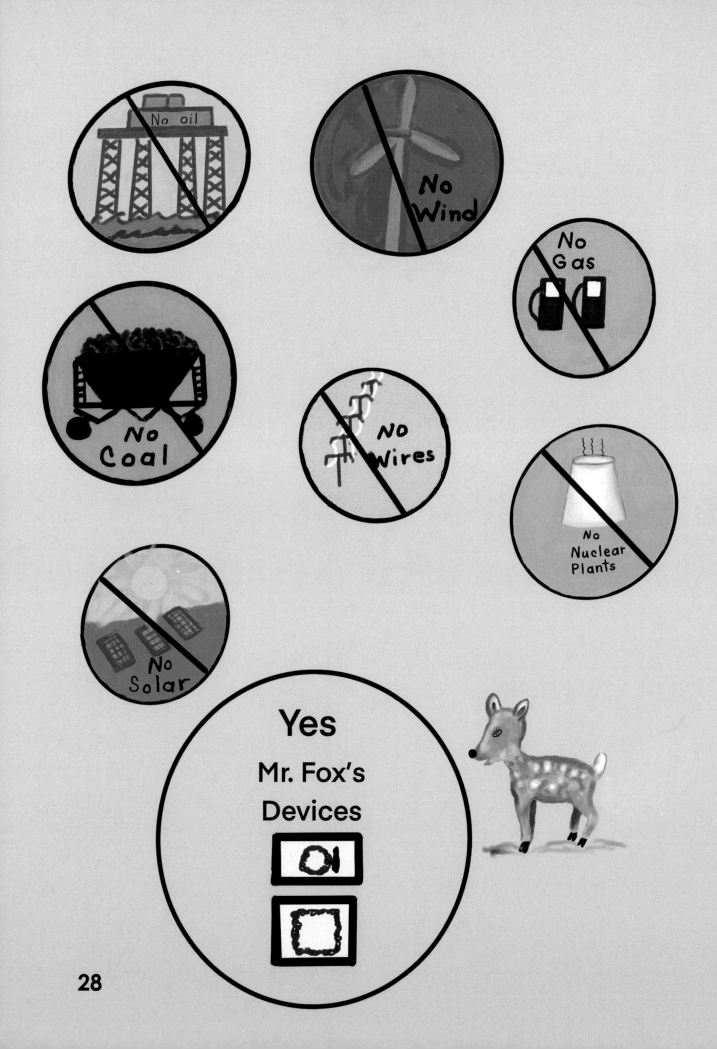

NATO

Greta Thunberg

How Dare You

Greta Thunberg has caused a tear
Saying, "A global strike is here."
At NATO's meeting of the world,
"Climate Youth Movement" was unfurled.
Climate activists wanted hype
Declaring global climate strike,
"Hundred percent renewable world."

Mr. Fox has found a new way.
His electricity's the key.
In electric cars, we will roam.
Continuous power for free.
Homes have free electricity.
Using fossil fuels need not be.
Move over climate change today.
Stop climate change for you and me.

Things I Can Do
to save the world

Recycle glass and plastics
Walk to a nearby park
Plant small gardens
Turn off water while brushing teeth
Use no plastic straws
Turn off lights when leaving the room
Use reusable bags
Buy less
Compost to decrease garbage